# Social Skills Activities
## for Today's Kids

**AGES 6-7**

Name:

## Note to Parents

The activities in this book are designed to help your child think about social skills and how they can be used in everyday life at the park, at school, or at a store, for example. Learning social skills will be an important part of your child having friendships and other meaningful relationships, as well as positive interactions with his or her peers.

Provide support as your child does the activities. Read the directions aloud and complete the activities together, discussing your child's feelings and thoughts. Answer any questions your child has. Learning social skills can be challenging, so being patient and providing support as your child learns how to apply what he or she has learned to relationships and social situations is an important part of your child's experience.

---

All illustrations and photography, including those from Shutterstock.com, are protected by copyright.

Editorial Development: Tiffany Hailey
Teera Robinson
Lisa Vitarisi Mathews
Copy Editing: Laurie Westrich
Art Direction: Yuki Meyer
Cover Illustration: Dana Regan
Illustration: Mary Rojas
Design/Production: Jessica Onken

**Evan-Moor®**
Educational Publishers

**EMC 3118**
**Congratulations on your purchase of some of the finest teaching materials in the world.**

*No part of this book may be reproduced in any form or stored in any retrieval system without the written permission of publisher.*

Evan-Moor Corporation
phone 1-800-777-4362, fax 1-800-777-4332.
Entire contents © 2023 Evan-Moor Corporation
10 Harris Court, Suite C-3, Monterey, CA 93940-5773. Printed in China.

CPSIA: Asia Pacific Offset Ltd, Kowloon, Hong Kong, China [9/2024]

# CONTENTS

## Making Friends

### Making New Friends — 8

Different Ways to Meet New Friends ....... 8
Would You Say Hi? ................................ 9
Saying Hello ........................................ 10
Talking with Your Body ........................ 11
Questions to Ask New Friends .............. 12
How to Be a Friend .............................. 13
Friendship Puppets .............................. 14
Practicing with Friendship Puppets ........ 17
New Friends Bingo .............................. 18

### Being a Good Friend — 19

Friendship Sundae .............................. 19
How to Be a Good Friend ..................... 20
Friendship Drawings ............................ 23
Friendship Card .................................. 24
Helping Hand ..................................... 27
Buddy Badges .................................... 28

### Playing at My House — 31

Do You Want to Come Over? ................ 31
What If My Friend Says No? .................. 32
We Do This at Our House ..................... 33
Backyard Fun ..................................... 34
Sharing Your Things with a Friend ......... 35
Do You Want a Snack? ......................... 36
Questions About "Do You Want a Snack?" .................................. 37
What Do You Like to Do? ..................... 38
Things I Do When I Have a Friend at My House ........................... 41

### Going to a Friend's House — 43

Sharing with a Friend .......................... 43
Eating with People .............................. 44
Talk with Your Family: Do I Need to Ask First? ........................ 47
Being a Guest .................................... 48

*Contents continue on the next page.*

# Being at School

## Classroom — 52

Classroom Rules .................... 52

Talking in the Classroom .................... 55

Your Turn to Talk .................... 56

Angry at School .................... 57

Is It a Good Choice? .................... 58

That's Mine .................... 59

Too Close? .................... 60

Healthy Habits .................... 61

Show and Tell .................... 62

Learning About People .................... 63

Talk with Your Family:
What Can I Bring? .................... 64

## Lunchtime — 65

Eating Together .................... 65

Can I Eat with You? .................... 66

Too Shy to Ask? .................... 67

Lunchtime Talk .................... 68

Talk with Your Family:
Is It Okay? .................... 69

## Playground — 70

Playground Rules .................... 70

Playing with Kindness .................... 73

Safe Playground Chart .................... 74

I Can Ask to Play .................... 77

How to Ask to Play .................... 78

Play with Others .................... 79

Angry on the Playground .................... 80

Bullying on the Playground .................... 81

Play by Myself .................... 82

## After School — 85

School Bus .................... 85

After-School Program .................... 86

Talk with Your Family:
Calling My Friends .................... 87

My Phone Number .................... 88

*Contents continue on the next page.*

# Going Places

## Out and About — 90

Saying Hello Can Be Hard ............... 90
Talking with People ............... 91
Wave Hello Art Project ............... 92
Talk with Your Family: Is It Okay? ......... 95
Seeing People ............... 96
Looking at People ............... 97
People with Disabilities ............... 98
Talking About People ............... 101
Use Your Voice! ............... 102
Listening to People ............... 103
How Close? ............... 104
Things I Like When I Go Out ............... 105

## People's Houses — 106

Going to People's Houses ............... 106

## Out with Pets — 108

Seeing People's Pets ............... 108
Out with a Dog ............... 109

## Restaurant — 110

Restaurant Rules ............... 110
Family Night Out ............... 111

## Store — 112

Rules in the Store ............... 112
Shopping Cart Safety ............... 115
Asking Questions in a Store ............... 116
Showing Respect in a Store ............... 117
Please and Thank You ............... 118
Excuse Me ............... 119
Touching People's Baskets ............... 120

## Handbook — 121

# Making Friends

Making friends can be fun.
There are things to think about when you are trying to make friends.
There are things to think about when you have a friend.

- ⭐ You think about how to say "hi" to meet new friends.
- ⭐ You think about how to talk with friends.
- ⭐ You think about how friends treat each other.
- ⭐ You think about what to do when you have friends at your house or when you go to friends' houses.

**Making New Friends**

Page 8

**Being a Good Friend**

Page 19

**Playing at My House**

Page 31

**Going to a Friend's House**

Page 43

# Different Ways to Meet New Friends

Making New Friends

You can meet new friends in different places.

Color the star if it tells a place where you can meet a new friend.

a place you go with your family

your neighborhood

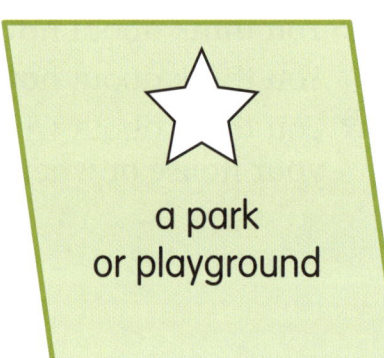
a park or playground

Write one place where you have met a friend. Then draw to show how you met your friend.

I met a new friend at _____.

# Would You Say Hi?

Making New Friends

Sometimes you might feel too shy to say **hi** or talk to kids.
Sometimes other kids might feel too shy to say **hi** to you.
Saying **hi** to new people is one way to make new friends.

Read. Then answer the items.

You and your family go to the pool. There are lots of kids.
They are playing together. They look happy.

Would you like to say **hi** to the kids?
Color the circle.

○ yes    ○ no

Circle the things you might say.

Can I play with you?

Hi, what are your names?

Your swim suit is cool.

# Saying Hello

Making New Friends

You see other kids when you go places.
Some kids say hello or wave. You may want to say hello, too.

Look at all the ways you can say hello.
Color the pictures that show ways you might want to say hello.

You can wave.

You can say **hi**.

You can do a fist bump.

You can look at the person and smile.

# Talking with Your Body

**Making New Friends**

Some people may not tell you how they feel, but their body can show it.

Look at each face. Write a word that tells the feeling for each face.

| happy    sad    mad    afraid |

_____    _____    _____

Look at both pictures.
Which girl wants to play?
Circle the picture.

Draw what you look like when you want to play.

# Questions to Ask New Friends

Making New Friends

Sometimes it can feel hard to talk to new friends.
Sometimes you might not know what to say.
You can ask your friends questions.
This can help you learn about your friends.

Read the questions.
Color the 😊 next to each question you can ask a friend.

 What is a game that you like to play?

 What is a TV show that you like?

 What pets do you have?

 What is a food that you like?

# How to Be a Friend

Making New Friends

One way to find a friend is to be a friend.

Read the poem. Then write rhyming words from the box to finish the poem.

> school    friend    hard

Nevaeh is making a card to send,

It is for her best _____.

She will also make another card,

She knows that making friends can be _____.

She will make it for the new kid at _____,

He might be her new friend, which would be cool!

Draw a picture of a card you would give to a new friend.

# Friendship Puppets

Making New Friends

Make puppets that you can play with.
You can use them to practice talking to other people.
You can use them to practice making new friends.

### What You Need

- pages 15 and 17
- crayons or markers
- scissors
- two lunch-sized paper bags
- glue
- materials such as colored construction paper, pompoms, yarn, chenille stems, dried pasta, etc.

### What You Do

1. Draw faces on page 15.
2. Cut out the faces you drew and glue one face to the bottom of each paper bag.
3. Next, draw a body on each paper bag to make a puppet.
4. Use materials to make hair for each puppet.
5. Use page 17 and your puppets to practice making new friends.

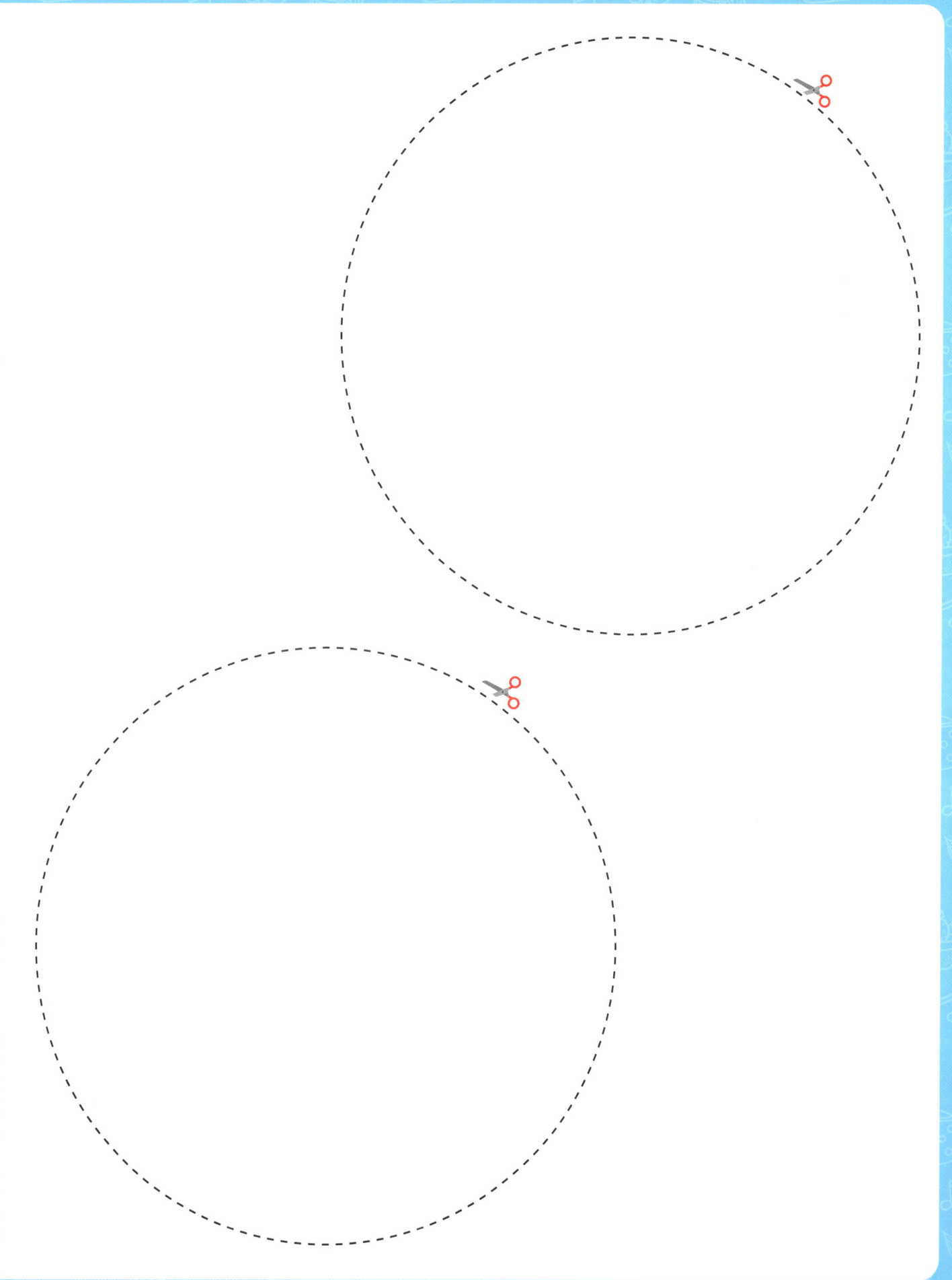

# Practicing with Friendship Puppets

Making New Friends

You can practice talking to people.
You can practice making new friends.

Use the puppets you made to practice talking to people. You can use the words below or your own words.

**Puppet 1 says:** Hi. I like your hair.

**Puppet 2 says:** Thanks. I like yours, too.

**Puppet 1 says:** Do you want to play?

**Puppet 2 says:** Okay. What is your name?

**Puppet 1 says:** My name is _____.

**Puppet 2 says:** My name is _____.

# New Friends Bingo

Making New Friends

There are many ways to make new friends.

Read the squares. Pick a square to do. After you do it, color the square. When you have colored all the squares, yell BINGO!

## BINGO

| | | |
|---|---|---|
| Say "hello" to someone new. | Ask someone new his or her name. | Help a new friend do something.  |
| Ask someone new if he or she wants to play with you. | Smile and wave at someone. | Share a toy with someone.  |
| Draw a picture for a new friend and give it to him or her.  | Say something kind, like "I like your shirt!" | Ask someone new to eat lunch with you.  |

# Friendship Sundae

Being a Good Friend

Friendships are nice to have—just like an ice cream sundae! Cut out the words in the cherries that tell why you are a good friend. Glue them onto the sundae. Then write a word to finish the sentence.

I am a good friend because I am _____.

kind   helpful   honest   fun

© Evan-Moor Corporation • EMC 3118 • Social Skills for Today's Kids

# How to Be a Good Friend

Being a Good Friend

There are many things you can do to be a good friend. Friends help each other. They listen to each other. They use kind words. They share and take turns.

Cut out the pictures on page 21. Find the pictures that match the sentences. Then glue one picture above each sentence. You will not use all the pictures.

| glue | glue |
|---|---|
| A good friend uses kind words. | A good friend listens. |

| glue | glue |
|---|---|
| A good friend helps. | A good friend shares and takes turns. |

# Friendship Drawings

Read the sentences. Then draw a picture to go with each sentence.

**Being a Good Friend**

Friends share.

Friends talk.

Friends play.

Friends help.

# Friendship Card

Being a Good Friend

Friends help each other. Friends use kind words. You can show your friend you care by making a card.

## What You Need

- page 25
- scissors
- markers

## What You Do

1. Cut out the card on page 25. Fold it in half.
2. Color the picture on the front of the card.
3. Write your friend's name on the top line inside of the card. Finish the sentence to tell why he or she is a good friend. Then write your name on the bottom line inside the card.
4. Give your friend the card with a smile.

24     Social Skills for Today's Kids • EMC 3118 • © Evan-Moor Corporation

# Friends Forever

--- fold ---

––––––––– fold –––––––––

Dear _____,

Thank you for being a good friend.
You are a good friend because you

_____

_____.

From,

_____

# Helping Hand

Being a Good Friend

A good friend is a good helper. You can give a helping hand to your friends. Draw a picture inside the hand that shows you helping your friend.

# Buddy Badges

Friends are buddies. Friends like to do some of the same things. Sometimes friends like to give each other things. Sometimes friends like to match.

You and your friend can wear matching Buddy Badges. Make matching badges for you and your friend to wear.

### What You Need

- page 29
- crayons or markers
- scissors
- glue
- tape or a safety pin

### What You Do

1. Think of something that you and your friend both like. Do you like soccer? Do you like music or skating?
2. Color and cut out pictures that match on page 29 if they show something you and your friend like. Glue each picture to a badge. Or you can draw your own matching pictures on the badges.
3. Give a badge to your friend. Keep one for yourself.
4. Use tape to stick the badge to your backpack, to your shirt, or anywhere else you want to put it. Or you can ask an adult to help you pin it on.
5. Use your badge when you want to match with your friend!

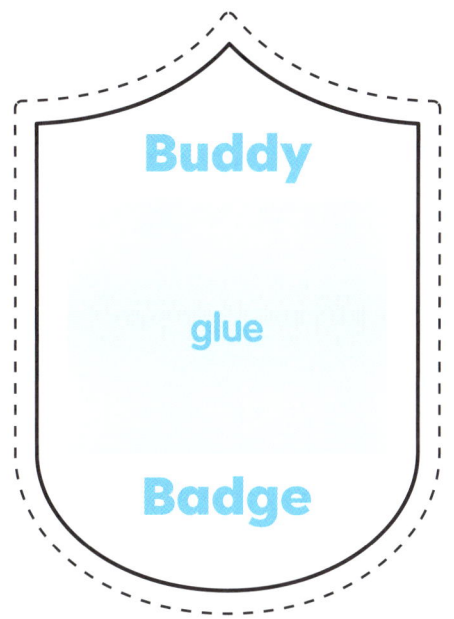
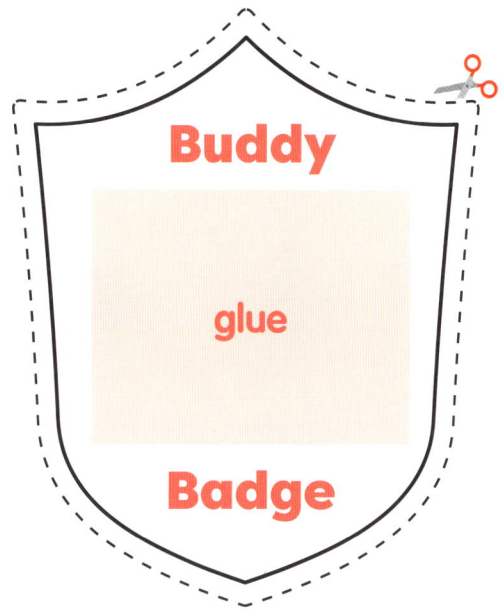

# Do You Want to Come Over?

Playing at My House

Friends like to spend time together.
Sometimes friends play at each other's houses.

Pretend that you want to invite your friend to play at your house. Draw a picture of yourself in the box. Then draw a line from your picture to the words you might say. Write one more thing you might say.

- It would be fun to play with you after school.

- I have some cool games at my house. Do you want to come over and play?

- Can you play after school sometime?

# What If My Friend Says No?

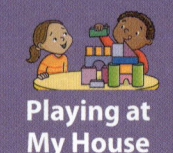

Playing at My House

Read. Then circle **yes** or **no** to answer the questions and tell what you think.

You ask your friend to come over to play. Your friend says no. He or she can't come over.

*I can't come over.*

Can you still have fun if your friend can't come over?    yes    no

Can you ask your friend to come over another day?    yes    no

Can you ask another friend to come over to play?    yes    no

# We Do This at Our House

Playing at My House

Families may have house rules, or things they do at their home.
Every family may have different house rules.
Some families may have the same house rules.

When you are at a friend's house, your friend may tell you how his or her family does things. Read about the house rules some people may have. Then draw a line to match the picture to the house rule.

We can play video games for one hour, then we can play outside.

There are snacks for us in the kitchen. We don't eat snacks in the living room.

We take our shoes off at my house. Can you take your shoes off, please?

# Backyard Fun

Read the story. Then answer the questions.

    Trevor invited his new friend Ryan over to play at his house after school. They ate snacks as soon as they got to Trevor's house, and then they went to the backyard to play. They put on baseball gloves and threw the ball back and forth. Next, they took out the soccer net and soccer ball and practiced kicking. After that, they rode skateboards on the patio. They had fun playing in Trevor's backyard.

    "Can we go inside and play video games now?" asked Ryan.

    "Sure," said Trevor, "we just have to put away everything we played with first."

    "Why?" asked Ryan. "We just leave everything out at my house so we can play with it the next day."

    "My mom likes for it all to be put away. It's one of the rules we follow at my house," said Trevor.

What do you think Ryan should do?

_____

_____

If you were Trevor, would you have told Ryan the rule about putting things away? Why or why not?

_____

_____

# Sharing Your Things with a Friend

Playing at My House

When you have a friend over to your house, there are toys and other things you want to share. There are also toys and other things you may <u>not</u> want to share.

Draw pictures of things you want to share when your friend is at your house. Then draw pictures of things you do <u>not</u> want to share.

**Things I will share with my friend**

**Things I do <u>not</u> want to share with my friend**

# Do You Want a Snack?

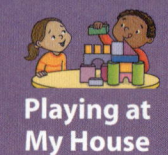

Sometimes friends like different things. Read the story about two friends who like to eat different kinds of snacks.

Lena was so happy that her friend Teera came over to her house to play.

First, they drew pictures. Then they made bead bracelets. After that, they played with Lena's cat, Kiwi. Lena was ready for a snack.

"Do you want a snack, Teera?" asked Lena.

"Okay," said Teera. "What kind of snacks do you have?"

"Well," said Lena, "we have bananas and granola bars."

Teera thought about how to answer Lena. She did not like bananas or granola bars. "Um, I guess I'm not that hungry," said Teera.

Lena could tell that her friend wanted a snack, but not those snacks.

"What snacks do you eat at your house?" asked Lena.

"I eat cheese and crackers. I eat baby carrots, too."

"I think we have baby carrots and crackers!" said Lena. She put them both on plates and gave them to Teera. Then she got two juice boxes out of the fridge. She knew Teera liked juice.

The friends sat at the table and ate their snacks. They talked about what they wanted to do next.

# Questions About "Do You Want a Snack?"

You read about Lena and her friend Teera.
Answer the questions about the story.

Did Lena and Teera like the same snacks?    yes    no

Circle the snacks that Lena likes.

Circle the snacks that Teera likes.

What did Lena do when Teera did not want a banana and a granola bar?

_____

_____

Circle the things you can do when you have a friend over to your house and you are going to have a snack.

- tell your friend the foods and drinks you have
- ask your friend what foods and drinks he or she likes
- put lots of snacks on a plate and let your friend choose

# What Do You Like to Do?

**Playing at My House**

When you have a friend over to your house, you can tell your friend what you like to do. You can also ask your friend what he or she likes to do. Friends can like different things.

1. Pretend you are having a friend over to play.

2. Cut out all of the pictures on page 39.

3. Glue the pictures in the squares to show what you like to do, what your friend likes to do, and what you both like to do!

| Things I like to do | Things my friend likes to do | Things we both like to do |
|---|---|---|
| glue | glue | glue |
| glue | glue | glue |

Remove and display where your child can see this chart.

# Things I Do
## When I Have a Friend at My House

Be kind.

Ask your friend what he or she would like to do.

Tell your friend the house rules when he or she needs to know them.

Think about your friend's feelings.

Think about which toys and games you want to play with your friends.

Ask your friend if he or she is hungry or thirsty.

Tell your friend things you like to do.

Have fun!

# Sharing with a Friend

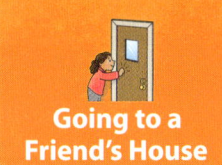
Going to a Friend's House

Look at the 2 pictures.
Draw an **X** on the picture that shows kids who are not sharing.

Circle the things you think are okay to share at a friend's house.

toy blocks

soup

your friend's special stuffed animal

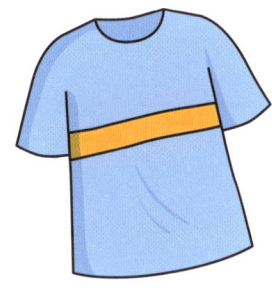
clothes

a blanket

grapes

# Eating with People

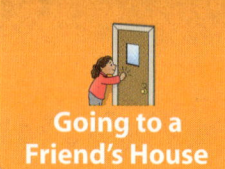
Going to a Friend's House

There are things that you might do when you eat with other people. Other people might do these things, too.

Cut out the pictures and sentences on page 45. Match each one to the picture or sentence it belongs with. Glue it below.

| glue |  |  |
|---|---|---|
| Wash your hands before you eat. | glue | glue |

| glue |  | glue |
|---|---|---|
| Wipe your hands and your mouth with a napkin. | glue | Bring your dish to the sink when you finish eating. |

| | |
|---|---|
| Don't reach over people. Ask them to pass the food you want. |  |
|  |  |
| Chew with your mouth closed. | Ask before taking more food. |

# Talk with Your Family

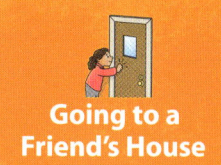
Going to a Friend's House

## Do I Need to Ask First?

Every family is different. The people in every house do things differently. Sometimes it is important to ask a grown-up before you do something. Think about how you do things in your home. Think about if you should do things the same way at a friend's house.

Read the list below with your parents. Draw an **X** in the box if you think you should ask a grown-up or your friend before you do each thing when you're at a friend's house.

- ☐ going inside your friend's parents' room
- ☐ feeding your friend's pet
- ☐ using the bathroom
- ☐ getting a snack from the kitchen cabinet
- ☐ eating food in a room that is not the kitchen
- ☐ taking a nap because you are tired
- ☐ leaving the house to talk with a neighbor
- ☐ using the computer
- ☐ cleaning up your mess

# Being a Guest

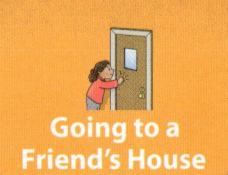

Going to a Friend's House

There are things you do when you are a guest at a friend's house. There are things you may not want to do, too.

## Things You Do

glue

glue

## Things You May Not Want to Do

glue

glue

Make a chart about being a guest. First, cut out the sentences below. Then glue each sentence on page 48 below the picture it matches.

| Get food without asking. | Put away the things you played with. |

| Say "thank you" to your friend for having you over. | Run in the house or climb on the furniture. |

Write three things you like about going to a friend's house.

**Things I like about going to a friend's house**

1. _____

2. _____

3. _____

# Being at School

**There are many things to think about when you are at school.**

⭐ You think about the things you need to do at school.
⭐ You think about how to talk to the kids and the grown-ups at school.
⭐ You think about who you want to play with at school.
⭐ You think about the rules at school.

Sometimes it is hard to know what to say and do when you are at school. Sometimes it can help to think about your feelings about rules, people, and things that happen at school and after school.

**Classroom**

Page 52

**Lunchtime**

Page 65

**Playground**

Page 70

**After School**

Page 85

# Classroom Rules

Classroom

There are rules you follow when you are at school.
Your classroom may have rules to follow.

glue

glue

glue

glue

glue

glue

# Classroom Rules

Make a classroom rules chart. First, cut out the sentences below. Then glue each sentence on page 52 below the picture it matches.

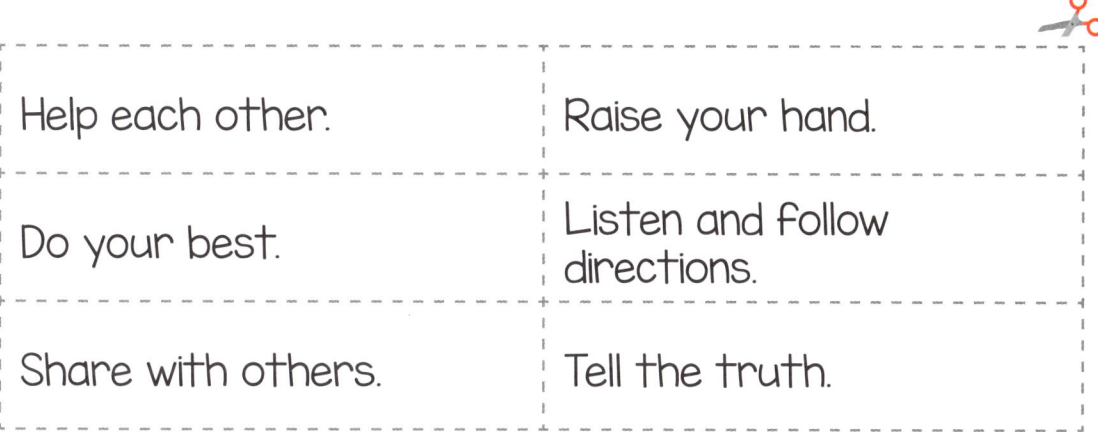

| Help each other. | Raise your hand. |
| Do your best. | Listen and follow directions. |
| Share with others. | Tell the truth. |

Write or draw 3 more classroom rules.

1.

2.

3.

# Talking in the Classroom

Classroom

Read each sentence in the chart.
Do you think each sentence tells something that is okay or not okay to do?
Draw a 🙂 or a ☹️ to tell what you think for each sentence.

| Read the sentence | Draw |
|---|---|
| I talk loudly while my teacher is reading to the class. | |
| I talk to my classmates quietly while we are waiting for our teacher. | |
| I talk to my classmates about soccer during the math lesson. | |
| I raise my hand and wait to be called on to ask a question. | |
| I talk to my friends during free play time. | |
| I do not talk during quiet time. | |

# Your Turn to Talk

Classroom

Sometimes you have to wait your turn to talk.

Read each story. Color the circle to answer the question.

You want to tell your teacher something, but she is talking to someone else. What do you do?

○ talk to your teacher anyway

○ wait until your teacher is finished

Your teacher is teaching a math lesson. You have a question about it. What do you do?

○ raise your hand

○ start talking while your teacher is talking

You are in a small reading group. You really like the story. Each person is taking turns reading one page. You want to read next, but it is not your turn. What do you do?

○ ask your teacher if you can go next

○ just start reading even if it is not your turn

○ wait until it is your turn to read

# Angry at School

 Classroom

Sometimes when you are at school, you may feel angry about something. There are things you can do when you feel angry.

Look at the picture. Read about it. Then color the picture.

Take deep breaths.

Talk to a friend.

Talk to your teacher.

Go to a quiet place.

# Is It a Good Choice?

You may feel angry when you are at school.
Even if you feel angry, you can still make good choices.

Read about the children who were angry at school.
Circle **yes** or **no** to tell if what they did was a good choice.

Will did not get a turn to use the tablet. He felt so mad. He yelled at his teacher, "It is not fair!" He threw a book on the ground. Was this a good choice?

 yes     no

Jalysia did not want to sit on the carpet to do the weather calendar. She wanted to keep drawing a picture. She felt so angry, so she pushed the crayons on the floor and stomped her feet. Was this a good choice?

 yes     no

Tyson needed a tissue. He put down the tablet he was using on his desk and went to get a tissue. When he came back, Blake was using the tablet. Tyson asked Blake to give it back, and Blake said, "I thought you were done. I have it now. I'm not going to give it back." Tyson felt angry. He took a few deep breaths. Then he went to talk to his teacher about what happened. Was this a good choice?

 yes     no

# That's Mine

Classroom

Sometimes there are many children in one classroom.
Each child brings things to school that belong to him or her.

Color the pictures that show things children bring to school.

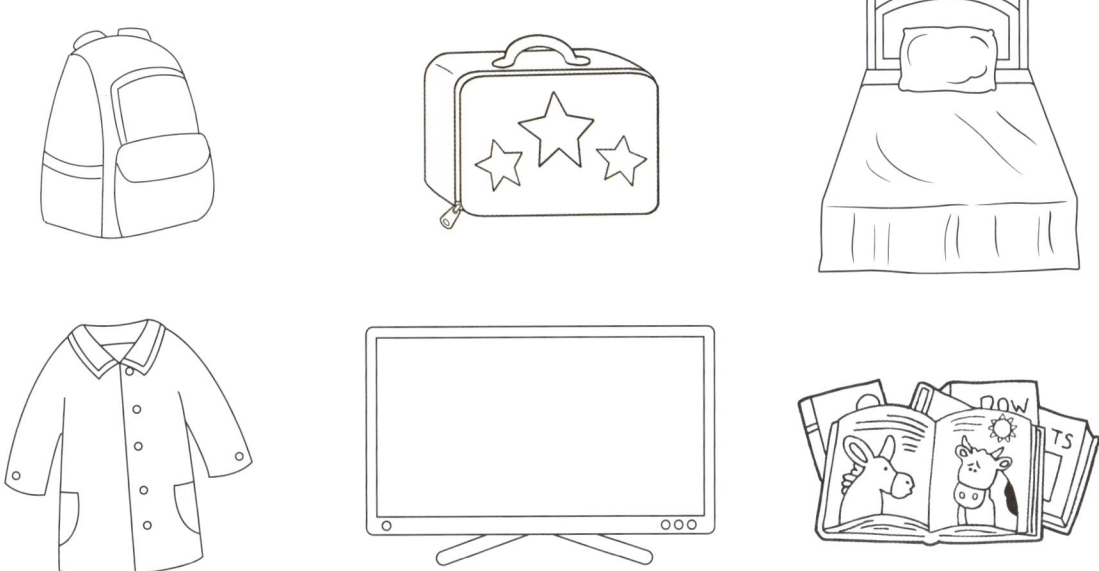

Is it okay for someone to touch your things?
Is it okay for you to touch someone else's things?
Think about the questions. Write **yes** or **no** to tell what you think.

| Is it okay if someone opens your backpack and takes something out of it? | _____ |

| Is it okay to pick up a jacket that is on the carpet and hang it on the hook? | _____ |

| Is it okay for you to open someone else's lunchbox and look inside it? | _____ |

# Too Close?

Classroom

Sometimes there are many children in one classroom.
Each child has his or her own space. You have your own space.

Read about how some children feel.
Think about how you feel.
Answer the questions.

Some children feel okay if you stand or sit close to them.

Some children do not like if you stand or sit close to them.

How do you feel if someone stands or sits close to you?
Write or draw to tell how you feel.

How do you feel if people touch you on your arm when they talk to you?
Is it okay? Or is it not okay? Write or draw to tell how you feel.

# Healthy Habits

Classroom

Sometimes there are many children in one classroom.
Sometimes people cough or sneeze.
Sometimes people need to blow their nose.

Write a √ for all the things that you and your classmates can do to try to keep each other healthy.

☐ cover your cough

☐ use a tissue

☐ wash your hands

☐ sneeze into your elbow

# Show and Tell

Your class may have a show-and-tell day. When you show something from your house, your classmates can learn more about you.

Draw 2 things from your house that you would like to show at school. Then finish the sentences.

I would like to show _____.

I would like to show _____.

# Learning About People

Classroom

When your classmates bring something from their house to show and tell about, you can learn about your classmates. You might learn how you are the same and different.

These are things your classmates may show and tell about. Draw a 😊 if it's something you want to know about your classmates.

foods they eat at home

games they play at home

stuff they have in their room or house

their family

books they like to read

special clothes they wear

# Talk with Your Family

Classroom

## What Can I Bring?

Some things are okay to bring to school. Some schools have rules about what you can bring. Your parents might have rules about what you can bring. Talk to your parents before you bring something for show and tell.

Read the questions below with your parents. Talk about the answers.

**?** Is there something I should not bring to school?

**?** Can I bring family pictures to school?

**?** Should I ask you before I put something in my backpack?

# Eating Together

Lunchtime

Sometimes people like to eat together.
There are things some people do when they eat together.

Circle the picture that tells about the sentence.

People chew with their mouths closed.

People use a napkin to wipe their mouths.

People talk when they don't have food in their mouths.

# Can I Eat with You?

Lunchtime

Sometimes you may want to eat lunch with someone at school.

Read the question.
Color the circle next to the question you might ask someone.

  ◯ Is it okay if I sit next to you?

  ◯ I like your lunchbox. Can I eat with you?

  ◯ Do you want to eat lunch together today?

# Too Shy to Ask?

Lunchtime

It can be hard to ask someone if they want to eat with you. You may feel too shy to ask. There are other things you can do.

Read. Write **yes** in the shapes that tell about things you feel like you can do. Then write your own idea in the triangle.

Say something kind to the person. You could say, "I like your shirt."

Say, "I'm glad it is time to eat!"

Look at the person and smile.

Write something else you might do.

# Lunchtime Talk

Lunchtime

People eat different foods at lunch.
Some people talk about what they are eating.

Read the sentence. Circle **yes** or **no** to tell if you might say this at lunchtime.

I am having tacos.
What are you having?

yes    no

I like eggs with rice.
Do you?

yes    no

I have not had that kind of sandwich before. What is it?

yes    no

# Talk with Your Family

Lunchtime

## Is It Okay?

Talk with your family to find out if these things are okay for you to do at lunchtime.

Read the questions below with your parents. Talk about the answers.

 Is it okay for me to share my food?

 Is it okay for me to ask someone to share his or her food with me?

 Is it okay for me to ask someone what he or she is eating?

# Playground Rules

Playground

Playground rules help everyone have fun and stay safe.

glue

glue

glue

glue

glue

glue

Make a playground rules chart. First, cut out the sentences below. Then glue each sentence on page 70 below the picture it matches.

| Stand in line and wait your turn. | Say kind words. |
| Play nicely together. | Play safely. Sit on the slide and swing. |
| Clean up your toys. | Tell an adult if someone is not following the rules. |

Write or draw 3 more playground rules.

1.

2.

3.

# Playing with Kindness

Playground

It is important to be kind on the playground. Being kind helps everyone have fun and stay safe.

Color the pictures that show kids being kind on the playground.

# Safe Playground Chart

Playground

Cut out the pictures on page 75.

Glue each picture below 😊 **safe** or 😟 **not safe** on this page to show if the kids in the picture are being safe on the playground.

| 😊 safe | 😟 not safe |
|---|---|
| glue | glue |
| glue | glue |
| glue | glue |
| glue | glue |

# I Can Ask to Play

Playground

You can ask someone if you can play with him or her.
Look at the person's eyes, smile, and use kind words.

Circle the child who looks like he wants to play.

Which picture shows a child who is using kind words? Color the circle.

Let me play, NOW!

○

That looks fun!
Can I play with you?

○

# How to Ask to Play

Playground

Deepa sees Ebony playing in the sandbox.
Deepa wants to play, too. But she does not know how to ask.

Help Deepa talk to Ebony.
Color all the squares that tell what she can say.

- [ ] Hello!
- [ ] That looks like fun!
- [ ] I love to play that game!
- [ ] Hi, Ebony!

What should Deepa say next?

Cut out the shapes at the bottom of this page.
Glue them to match the shapes and help Deepa ask Ebony to play.

glue △   glue ◇   glue ⬡   glue ◯   glue ▢

with   Can   you?   I   play

# Play with Others

Playground

Circle the things you like to do.
Then draw a picture of yourself playing with your friends.

| play ball | run | dance | play in the sand |

Cut out the words at the bottom of this page.
Glue them to match the colors and tell one way to ask others to play.

| glue | glue | glue | glue | glue | glue | glue |

| to | want | me? | Do | you | with | play |

# Angry on the Playground

Playground

Everyone feels angry sometimes.
When you feel angry, you can do things to try to feel better.

Color the pictures that show what you can do when you feel mad.

kick or throw a ball

have some quiet time

tell a teacher or a friend how you feel

count to 10

blow on your fingers like a candle

# Bullying on the Playground

Playground

Sometimes people act like bullies.
They say and do things that hurt others.

Look at the pictures. Trace the words that tell what you can do if you see bullying on the playground.

I can say, "__Stop__!"

I can __tell a teacher__.

I can try to __help__.

# Play by Myself

Playground

Sometimes you may not want to play with other people.
You can tell a friend in a nice way that you want to play by yourself.

Look at the pictures. Cut out the puzzle pieces on page 83.
Glue the puzzle pieces that tell kind ways to say that you want to play by yourself.

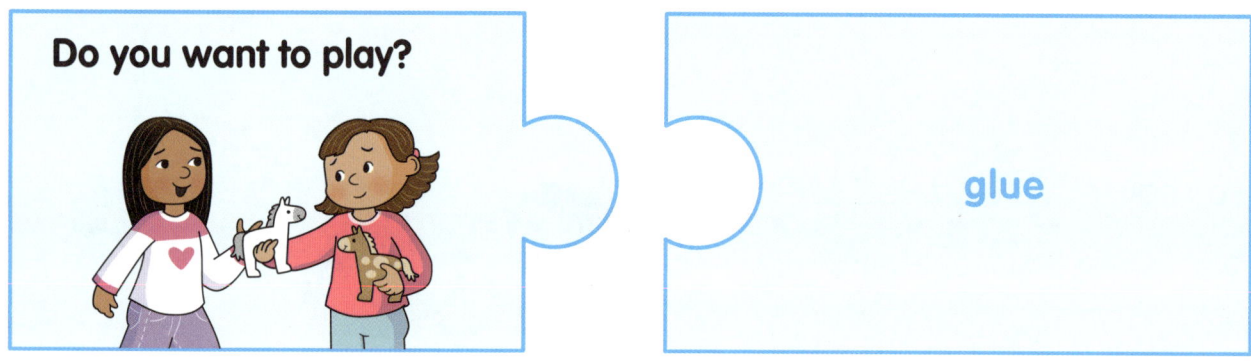

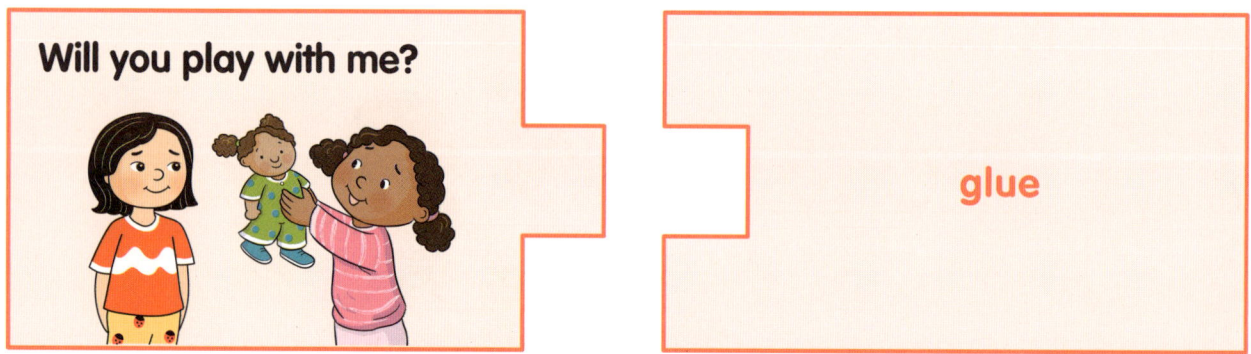

No, thank you.

Leave me alone!

Maybe next time.

I never want to play with you!

I don't want to play!

Sorry, I want to play by myself today.

# School Bus

After School

When you ride on a school bus, you can make choices. You can choose to be safe. You can choose to sit alone or with other people.

Look at the pictures and read the sentences.
Then color the circle to choose the sentence that tells about you.

○ I would rather stand when the bus is moving.

○ I would rather sit when the bus is moving.

○ I would rather talk to someone.

○ I would rather not talk.

# After-School Program

After School

Some kids go to a place with other kids after school.
They spend time there until their parents pick them up.
Kids can do a lot of things after school.

Look at the pictures. Read the sentences.
Then draw a line to match each sentence to a picture.

Kids can do art together.

A kid can be alone.

Kids can play together.

Kids can eat together.

# Talk with Your Family

After School

## Calling My Friends

Sometimes you may want to talk to your friends after school. You can ask your parents if it is okay. You might want to use their phone.

Ask your parents if you can use their phone to talk to your friends after school. Read the questions below with your parents. Talk about the answers.

 Is it okay to talk to my friends on the phone?

 Which phone can I use?

 Can I ask my friends for their phone numbers?

 Can you ask my friends' parents if I can call my friends?

 Can I give our phone number to my friends at school?

# My Phone Number

After School

If your parents say it is okay to talk to your friends on the phone, then you may want to tell your friends your phone number. Ask your parents what your phone number is.
Color the numbers on each phone below.

**first number**

**second number**

**third number**

**fourth number**

**fifth number**

**sixth number**

Write the seventh number.

Now write your phone number. _____

88     Social Skills for Today's Kids • EMC 3118 • © Evan-Moor Corporation

# Going Places

**There are many things to think about when you go places.**

⭐ You think about if it is okay to say "hello" to people you see.
⭐ You think about the rules at different places you go.
⭐ You think about how to act around other people's pets.
⭐ You think about how to act at a restaurant or a store.

You might go places with your family. You might go places with your friends. You see people when you go places. Some places have rules. Some places might not have rules. You can think about your choices when you go someplace.

**Out and About**

Page 90

**People's Houses**

Page 106

**Out with Pets**

Page 108

**Restaurant**

Page 110

**Store**

Page 112

# Saying Hello Can Be Hard

Out and About

People say hello to other people when they go places.
Saying hello may be hard for some people to do.
Saying hello may be easy for some people to do.

Color the star in all the circles that tell how you feel.

I feel shy when a grown-up I don't know says hello to me.

I like to meet new people. It is not hard for me to say hello.

It is hard for me to look at people in their eyes.

I like to smile at people and wave when I go places.

Some days I do not feel like talking to people.

I feel scared to say hello to kids I don't know. Maybe they won't like me.

# Talking with People

Out and About

Some people like when other people stand close to talk to them. Other people do not like to stand close. Some people like when other people talk loudly. Some people do not like it.

How close do you like other people to stand when they talk to you? Draw a picture of a person in one of the bubbles to show how close.

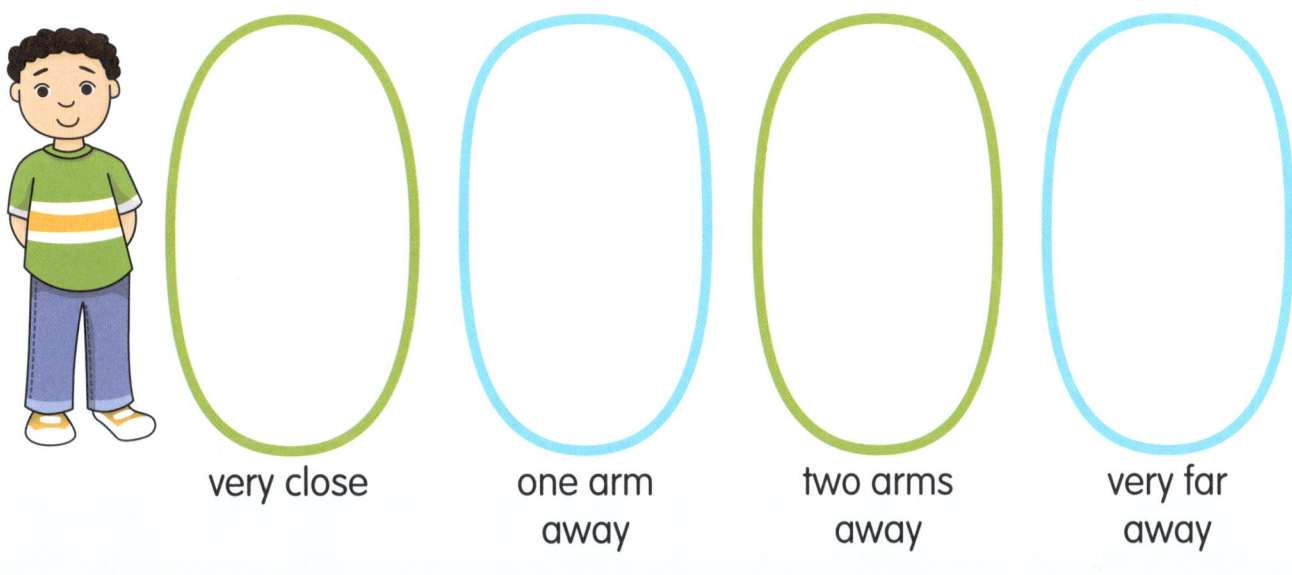

How loud do you think you should talk to people? Color your answer.

# Wave Hello Art Project

Out and About

Make a hand that you can use to wave hello.

### What You Need

- page 93
- scissors
- crayons or markers
- tape or glue
- craft stick

### What You Do

1. Draw a picture or write a word such as **hello** or **hi** on one side of the hand on page 93.
2. Use crayons or markers to color the other side of the hand.
3. Cut out the hand picture.
4. Use tape or glue to put the hand picture on a craft stick.
5. Bring the hand on a stick with you when you go somewhere and use it to wave hello to people.

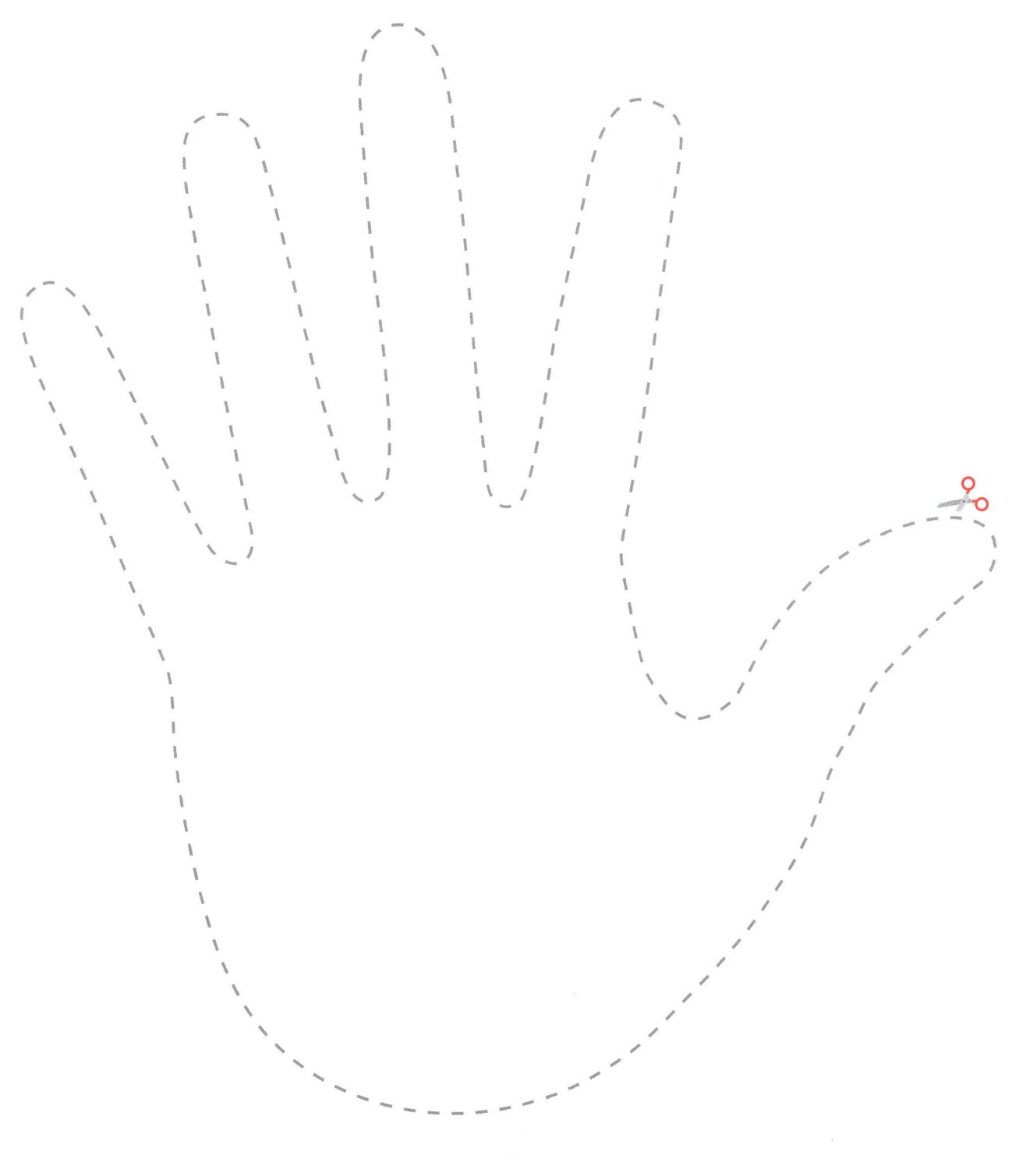

# Talk with Your Family

**Out and About**

## Is It Okay?

Talk with your parents to find out when it is okay to talk to people you don't know.

Read the questions below with your parents. Talk about the answers.

*hi!* Is it okay for me to say "hi" to someone I don't know?

*hi!* Is it okay for me to talk to a kid if he or she starts talking to me?

*hi!* Is it okay for me to talk to a grown-up in a store?

# Seeing People

Out and About

You see many people when you go places. Every person looks different. You may see a person who is not like anyone you have seen before.

Look at the pictures. Every person looks different.

Color the squares next to things you might do when you see a person who looks different than anyone you have seen before.

☐ smile at that person     ☐ look at that person, but not for too long

☐ wonder about that person     ☐ ask your parent about that person

☐ think, "maybe that person has not seen anyone like me before, either"

# Looking at People

Out and About

You see many people when you go places.
Every person looks different. Some people may have disabilities.
Some people understand that you may have questions about them.
Some people may have questions about you, too.

Read the story. It tells how two kids met each other.

> Reggie was riding his bike in front of his house. He saw a girl in a wheelchair ride by on the other side of the street. She was going pretty fast. Reggie stopped riding his bike and watched her ride up and down the street. He had never seen a wheelchair going so fast! All of a sudden, the girl rode across the street toward Reggie. "Hi, I'm Tracy," she said. "I saw you looking at me."
>
> "Yeah, sorry," said Reggie. "I did not mean to stare at you. You just looked so cool riding so fast up the street. Is it okay if I ask why you need a wheelchair?"
>
>
>
> "Yes, it's okay," said Tracy. "I can't move my legs at all, so I cannot walk or ride a bike. I use a wheelchair instead. Do you want to race down the street?" asked Tracy.
>
> "Sure!" said Reggie as he jumped on his bike.

Write a ✓ in the box next to all the things Reggie did that you would do, too.

☐ Reggie said he was sorry for staring at Tracy.

☐ Reggie asked Tracy if it was okay to ask her why she uses a wheelchair.

☐ Reggie jumped on his bike to race Tracy.

# People with Disabilities

**Out and About**

You see many people when you go places.
You may see some people who have disabilities.
There are many different disabilities.

These pictures show people who have different disabilities.

There are important things to know about people who have disabilities.
Cut out the boxes on page 99. Glue them in the boxes below.
Then read about people who have disabilities.

| glue | glue | glue |
|------|------|------|
| glue | glue | glue |

| Just because a person has a disability, it does not mean that person needs help. | People who have disabilities can do many things. |
| --- | --- |
| People who have disabilities may do things differently. | Some people do not like to talk about their disability. |
| There are disabilities you can see and disabilities you cannot see. | Some people do not mind if you ask them questions about their disability. |

# Talking About People

Out and About

When you go places, you may want to talk about people you see. You might have questions about people. You might want to say things about the people you see. It is important to make sure you do not say or do something that can hurt another person's feelings.

Read the sentences. Draw a ☺ or a ☹ below the sentences to tell how a person may feel if it happened to him or her.

- A boy told me he liked the striped wheels on my wheelchair.

- Someone pointed at me and laughed.

- A girl whispered to her friend that my hair looks weird.

- A man told me he likes my freckles— he had freckles, too!

- A kid asked me why I don't have two arms. I told him I was born with one arm. Then we played together on the slide.

# Use Your Voice!

Out and About

Sometimes you may want to use your loud voice. Other times, you may want to use your quiet voice. Think about how other people may feel.

Read about each place. Then answer the questions.

People go to the library to read and study.

People go to the park to play!

People go to the movie theater to see and hear a movie.

Circle the answer. Do you think it is better to talk quietly or loudly at…

 the library?

 the park?

 the movie theater?

# Listening to People

Out and About

We can show that we care about people when we listen to them.

Read the questions. Circle **yes** or **no**.

Do you think it's important to listen when a person is talking to you?

    **yes**    **no**

Is it hard for you to listen to people who are talking to you?

    **yes**    **no**

Look at the picture. It shows a girl and her brother at the beach. The girl is trying to tell her brother something, but he's not listening. Write answers to the questions.

What can the girl do to get her brother to listen to her?

_____

What can her brother do to be a better listener?

_____

# How Close?

Out and About

When you go places, you might see other people. Sometimes you may want to be close to them. Sometimes you may not want to be close to them.

Draw pictures to answer the questions.
Draw yourself in each picture.

How close do you like to stand to grown-ups you do not know at the store?

How close do you like to stand to your family at the store?

# Things I Like When I Go Out

Out and About

Read the sentences.
They tell about things that some people like when they go out.

Color the 👍 if you like what the sentence tells about.

Color the 👎 if you do not like it.

**thumbs up or down?**

| | | |
|---|---|---|
| I like when someone helps me reach something. | 👍 | 👎 |
| I like when people hold the door open for me and my family. | 👍 | 👎 |
| I like when people smile at me. | 👍 | 👎 |
| I like when people wave hello to me. | 👍 | 👎 |
| I like when people let me pet their dog. | 👍 | 👎 |

# Going to People's Houses

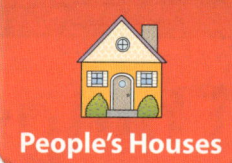
People's Houses

Sometimes people have rules for inside their house.
When you go to people's houses, they might want you to follow their rules.
The rules might be different from your house.

Read the house rules below. Cut them out.
Then glue each rule on page 107 below the picture it matches.

| | |
|---|---|
| Please do not feed the pets. | Please do not put your feet on the table. |
| Please hang your coat on the hook. | Please put your dirty dishes in the sink. |
| Wash your hands before you eat. | Please wipe your feet. |

glue

glue

glue

glue

glue

glue

# Seeing People's Pets

Out with Pets

If you have a pet, do you take it outside?
If you do not have a pet, do you like to see people with their pets?
Some people do not like to go near other people's pets, and some people do.

Look at the picture.

Do you think the girl likes to go near other people's dogs?
Write **yes** or **no**. _____

The sentences below tell what people can say if they see a person with a dog. Draw an **X** inside the circles that have a kind sentence.

- Sorry, I do not feel well when I am near a dog.
- Keep that animal away from me!
- Can I please pet your dog?

# Out with a Dog

Out with Pets

People can do things to help people feel okay around their dogs. People can do things to help dogs and their owners feel okay, too.

Read what people can say. Color the 😊 if you think it helps people feel safe. Color the 😟 if you think it does not help people feel safe.

I can have my dog wear a leash when we go on a walk.

I can have my dog run with no leash.

I can ask the dog owner if I can give the dog a treat.

I can feed another person's dog without asking.

# Restaurant Rules

Restaurant

Many people eat at restaurants.
Just like at school and at home, there are rules to follow at a restaurant.

Read the restaurant rules. Draw a ✓ next to the rules you follow at a restaurant.

## Restaurant Rules

- ☐ Say "please" and "thank you."
- ☐ Do not run.
- ☐ Use your inside voice.
- ☐ Stay at your own table.
- ☐ Go to the restroom with a grown-up.
- ☐ Try to keep your food on your plate.
- ☐ Do not touch other people's plates.
- ☐ Chew with your mouth closed.
- ☐ Use a napkin.

# Family Night Out

Restaurant

Circle the picture that matches the sentence.

My family and I eat at a restaurant.

We use our inside voices to talk about what we will order.

We say "thank you" when the server brings us our food.

I do not talk with my mouth full. I chew with my mouth closed.

# Rules in the Store

 Store

Some stores have rules to help everyone stay safe.
When you follow the rules, you show other people respect and kindness.

Cut out the pictures on page 113.
Glue them below if they show people being safe or being kind.

## I can follow the store rules

| glue | glue | glue |

| glue | glue |

# Shopping Cart Safety

Store

Draw a line to the 🛒 if you think the picture shows a person using the shopping cart safely.

sitting in cart

running

hitting people or things

walking

standing in cart

saying "excuse me"

# Asking Questions in a Store

Store

Read the question on each bag. Is it okay to ask a grown-up in a store that question? Color the bag handles if you think it is okay.

Can you help me find what I need?

Do you have kids?

Do you want to play with me in the store?

Where is the restroom?

Why are you dressed funny?

How much does that cost?

# Showing Respect in a Store

We can do things in a store to show other people respect and kindness. We can show respect by covering our mouths when we sneeze or cough. We can show respect by washing our hands after we use the bathroom. We can show respect by using a tissue to clean our nose.

Look at the pictures. Draw a line to help the child show respect to the other people in the store.

"I don't need to wash my hands."

# Please and Thank You

Store

You can say **please** when you ask for something.
You can say **thank you** when someone does something for you or gives you something.

Look at the pictures. Read the words the kids say to the workers. Then trace the words.

please

please

thank you

thank you

# Excuse Me

Store

You can say **excuse me** when you need to talk to someone.
You can also say it when you move past a person or when you burp.

Cut out the pictures. Then glue the pictures to match the sentence.

I say **excuse me** when I need to talk to my mom.

glue

---

I say **excuse me** when I need to move past a person.

glue

---

I say **excuse me** when I burp.

glue

---

# Touching People's Baskets

Read. Then answer the items.

Abdul found the last toy train in the store. He put it in his basket. Then he walked away to find a toy for his sister. But when he went back to his basket, the train was gone! Someone took his train!

Color the picture that shows how Abdul felt when someone took the train out of his basket.

 happy     sad

Do you think it is okay to touch things in other people's baskets?

 yes     no

Tell why or why not.

_____

_____

Note: Cut apart the pages. Put them in order. Staple them together.

# My Social Skills Handbook

# CONTENTS

Making Friends

Page 2

Being at School

Page 6

Going Places

Page 10

© Evan-Moor Corporation • EMC 3118 • Social Skills for Today's Kids

# You are learning about social skills. Good for you!

Learning about social skills can help you make friends. It can also help you think about what to do and how to act when you go to school. Learning about social skills can help you feel okay when you go to places like restaurants and stores.

You can look at this handbook to remind you of what you learned about social skills.

## Saying Hello

You can make a new friend by saying hello.

You can wave.

You can say **hi**.

You can look at the person and smile.

# Being a Good Friend

There are things you can do to be a good friend. A good friend . . .

shares and takes turns      listens      uses kind words

# Going to a Friend's House

There are things you do when you are a guest at a friend's house.

Ask before you get food.      Put away things that you played with.      Say **thank you** to your friend for inviting you over.

# Having a Friend Over

When you have a friend over, you can do things you both like to do.

Play games.

Make things.

Play outside.

# Following Rules at School

When you go to school, there are rules you follow.

Play safely.

Wait your turn to talk in class.

Keep your hands and feet to yourself in line.

# Making Good Choices at School

There are things you can do when you feel angry or sad at school.

 Take deep breaths.

 Talk to someone.

 Count to 10.

# Playing with Kids at School

There are many ways to ask other kids if they want to play with you.

 Can I play with you?

 Do you want to play?

 Will you play with me?

# Eating with Kids at School

There are things you do when you eat at school.

You can ask someone to eat with you.

Eat your own lunch.

Don't talk with your mouth full.

# Thinking About What to Do

There are things to think about when you go places.

if you are at a place where you should talk quietly

if you should touch or feed other people's pets

if you should talk to a person you don't know

# Having Healthy Habits

It is important to have healthy habits when you go places.

Use a tissue.

Cover your cough and sneeze.

Wash your hands.

# Eating at a Restaurant

There are things you can do when you are at a restaurant.

Say **thank you** when the server brings you your food.

Use a quiet voice.

Use a napkin to wipe your mouth.

# Shopping at a Store

There are rules to follow when you are at a store.

Do not run in the store.　　Pay for your things.　　Say **excuse me**.